Living through Grief

Jennifer Minney

with illustrations by
Brian Minney

Silvertree Publishing

Published 2002
by
Silvertree Publishing
PO Box 2768, Yeovil, Somerset

ISBN: 0-9538446-6-8

Printed and bound by
Creeds the Printers, Broadoak, Bridport, Dorset DT6 5NL

GRIEF

My darling's gone,
    but the trees are lovely still,
Startling in autumn beauty, just the same
As always, spreading their warmth as colours spill
To earth in dazzling drifts of gold and flame.
Why are the trees not bare, and cold the ground?
How can such vibrant beauty still be found
    when my love is dead and gone?

My darling's gone,
    but the sun still shines above,
Beaming its radiant light across the sky
As cloudlets race the wind on wings of love,
Their feathered whiteness sparkling as they fly.
Why are the clouds not black with heavy rain?
Why don't they share my puzzlement and pain,
    for my love is dead and gone?

My darling's gone,
    but there's movement in the street
As neighbours gossip still, and children play,
And workers still commute, and lovers meet,
And all of life goes on, as if the day
Were normal. Why don't they stop, this swirling throng?
For life without my love seems strange and wrong,
    and I too feel dead and gone.

JM (1979)

LIVING THROUGH GRIEF

THE STAGES OF GRIEF

The First Shock

Death always comes as a shock, however long it has been expected. The mind goes numb, unable to take in the dreadful fact that a loved one has gone forever. When the relationship has been a close one, or when death has not been anticipated, the sense of shock can be so profound that one is left feeling lost and bewildered, and incapable of performing the most basic tasks. On the other hand, you may walk away from the scene of death and carry on as usual, as if nothing has happened.

Both these reactions are a normal part of grieving. If you were severely injured physically you would not at first be aware of pain, because the nerve endings go into spasm, preventing any feeling from reaching the brain. A similar process occurs when the trauma is emotional. The "nerves" of your soul shut down, so the pain isn't registered. Therefore, if in the first impact of grief you wandered around like a lost and helpless child, this does not mean that you are inadequate, or that you were about to have a breakdown. And if you automatically resumed a half-finished household chore, it does not mean that you are heartless and uncaring. In either case, you were acting just as anyone might who has been cruelly separated from a beloved companion.

As well as being in a state of shock, there is at first no time to grieve. There is the funeral to organise, people to notify, and tasks that need immediate attention. And during this time family and friends flock around, eager to help in any way they can. If you are a church member, you may also have experienced that amazing sense of being wrapped around with love that comes from being constantly thought about and prayed for. And you might have been lulled into thinking that you are alright, that death is easier to bear than you imagined. And then, usually in a week or two, the numbness wears off, and the yearning begins. But this too is normal. It is the start of the next and most difficult phase of grief.

The Ongoing Struggle

It often happens that, after the funeral, the friends who have been such a help and comfort start drifting away, and you are left alone. But it is then, as the emotional pain really begins to be felt, that you need them most. The pain is experienced in different ways, depending on one's personality and typical ways of coping, and on the type of bereavement. Some forms of loss are more traumatic than others, and give rise to different kinds of feelings.

The death of a spouse or partner is especially devastating, although divorce can be more wounding because, with this, there is also a feeling of failure or rejection, as well as a sense of betrayal. Losing a child or young sibling, who should have had all of life before them, is extremely difficult to accept and can create tremendous anger and resentment. And if your loved one died violently, through accident, homicide or suicide, you will feel far more disturbed than if he or she died peacefully in bed. But whatever the type of loss and however it occurred, the yearning and searching for the departed, with the associated anger and feelings of guilt and fear, will eventually give way to depression.

Depression is a typical reaction to loss and can be described as the soul hurting. It is, therefore, to be expected. The soul-hurt, or sadness, is often manifested in apathy and indifference, which may worsen as you become increasingly aware of your loneliness. You may also feel disorientated, not really knowing where you belong anymore, and you could find yourself wondering if you will ever be happy again.

But grief does pass, although the duration, as well as the intensity, varies. In the case of a spouse it can take up to two years to recover. But during this time the pain should be diminishing, and there should be less-powerful yearnings for the loved one's return, with increasingly longer periods of freedom from the overwhelming sorrow and despair. There should also be a reduction of the physical symptoms that accompany depression, such as insomnia, constant tiredness, and vague aches and pains. And, long before you come to the end of the tunnel, you should start seeing glimmers of hope.

The Glimmers of Hope

The glimmers of hope are just that: tiny glimpses of light in the darkness. There is, during this phase of grief, no sudden walking into the noonday sun and discovering that the world is bright and beautiful again. You just keep on going, living one day at a time, trying to keep the light in view. Sometimes it beckons cheerfully and you rush expectantly towards it. Then, suddenly, it disappears, leaving you once again feeling lost and bewildered. But each time the light returns it is larger and brighter, and it remains for longer periods as life increasingly takes on a new meaning and purpose.

During those times when you are again plunged into darkness, it is some comfort to know that these setbacks are part of the normal grieving process. They do not necessarily mean that you have got stuck. Sometimes you will know why the darkness has deepened; at other times there will be nothing you can pinpoint as being the cause of the regression. Christmas and other special occasions are very difficult to cope with, especially

the first anniversary of the death, and you might find yourself right back at the start, not really believing that your beloved is no longer there. A chance word, an evocative smell, an old photograph – any of these can set you back for a while, triggering feelings you thought you had worked through. It helps, then, to remind yourself that there have been glimmers of light, and that the light will return.

Acceptance and Readjustment

While you are in the throes of grief, holding on to every little spark of hope, it is hard to imagine coming out of the tunnel and seeing the sun again. But the day will come when you can accept that your loved one is gone for ever, and readjust to a very different kind of life. This coincides with a feeling of being back in control, and with a new sense of belonging. If you have lost a spouse or partner, you will now be able to attend social gatherings and not feel like a misfit. If it is a child you have lost, you will find that you can tolerate being around pregnant women or other people's children and not have to brace yourself to ward off the expected stab of anguish. You will also experience renewed optimism as you confidently face a future that is bright with promise.

This final stage of grieving involves letting go and, as healing occurs, making a new start, with new hopes and new dreams. You will, of course, never forget your loved one. But life will again be full, and you will know once more what it is to be happy and content.

When Grief Won't Go

It sometimes happens that a bereaved person gets stuck in the grieving process, unable to move on. The sense of unreality and numbness may continue, with no sign of abating. There could be a persistent refusal to accept that the loved one will not return, perhaps with attempts to make time stand still – as with Miss Havisham in Dickens' *Great Expectations*. And sometimes, the normal reactive depression that is a part of grieving gets out of hand. If the depression is disproportional to the cause or lasts longer than expected, if it keeps you from functioning, or if there are constant thoughts of suicide, then it is classed as clinical. This simply means that medical intervention is required, perhaps in the form of antidepressants, counselling or other psychiatric help.

Depression is likely to become clinical if the loss has been very traumatic, if there has been a series of losses, or if the death has triggered unresolved issues from the past. Especially vulnerable are those who, for any reason, experienced the loss of a secure and loving environment in childhood. If the deceased was a parent who was abusive, neglectful or overly critical, then the death is bound to generate very confused and disturbed feelings. And if, as a result of past unhappiness, you have a tendency to blot out painful or negative emotions, depression has a far greater chance to take hold.

However, a bereavement often acts also as a catalyst, bringing repressed feelings to the surface. This makes it possible for old wounds, as well as the new, to start healing. You can facilitate this process, and thereby move yourself forward, by accepting and putting names to the morass of emotions that constitute grief, and by finding constructive ways of expressing them.

THE FEELINGS OF GRIEF

Yearning

Grief is not just one feeling, but a combination of feelings, sometimes experienced in succession; at others, all mixed up together. In the early stages especially, the predominant emotion is a yearning for the loved one's return. This can be very intense, and you may find yourself thinking that the deceased is still alive and, at any moment, will walk through the door. You may even imagine that you have heard your beloved's voice, or sensed a familiar presence. These sensations are very common, and no cause for alarm. They are also not surprising. We all internalise – take in and incorporate into our own being – the thoughts, feelings and attributes of others, especially those close to us. And healing comes, in part, from having worked through the grief and recognised that the loved one, in a sense, is still there. But the grief process cannot be short-circuited; and, until healing occurs, the yearning for the one you have lost can seem at times unbearable.

What you miss most will depend on your relationship with the departed and on your own needs. For instance, if it is a parent who has died, your greatest need may be for someone to turn to for advice or encouragement, or a shoulder to cry on. And the younger and more dependent you are, the more acutely you will feel your loss. When it is a partner who has been taken, you can find yourself longing for company, most noticeably in the evenings, and wanting someone to share things with. You might experience sexual cravings, or long for a warm body to snuggle up to at night, or a pair of arms around you. Or perhaps you will most miss having someone around the house taking care of all the little repair jobs, attending to the finances, or helping with the children. If the deceased was a baby or child, your greatest need might be for someone to hold or care for, and you will most miss

your daily routines, the baby smells or the sound of youthful chatter. You can even find yourself missing the deceased's annoying little habits, wishing you had someone to pick up after, to yell at to turn the stereo down, or to prod in the back to stop the snoring. But whatever form your yearning takes, it helps to be able to talk about it. And you must allow yourself to cry. Tears release the harmful chemicals that are formed in the body during times of stress, and bring healing and relief.

Anger

The yearnings that are a part of grief inevitably give rise to anger. And the most anger might be directed at the deceased, even though rationally you know that he or she did not choose to die – unless it was a suicide. Coping with a suicide is particularly difficult and creates a tremendous amount of anger, although this is often denied or suppressed. People who kill themselves do so usually because they are so depressed they can no longer think clearly, and they become convinced that suicide is the only way to escape unbearable emotional pain. They do not, as a general rule, intend to hurt the ones they leave behind, although of course they do – very much so. And hurt and anger always go together.

The same intense anger can be sparked by any avoidable death, such as that resulting from smoking or taking drugs and, of course, from homicide, in which case you will naturally be very angry with the killer. But even when the death is from natural causes, you may be angry because your loved one left you alone, because of the emotional pain you are experiencing, because of the resulting financial or practical difficulties, or because you have the unenviable task of comforting your children for the loss of a parent or sibling. Being angry with the deceased is not an indication of lack of love. On the contrary! The more you love someone, the more angry you are likely to feel at the seeming abandonment.

You might also be angry at yourself, or with doctors and nurses, for having failed to prevent the death, even if you know that nothing more could have been done. You may be angry with family members or friends who didn't rally round. You may even be angry with God. But, however irrational these causes of anger, they too are a natural response to bereavement and loss; they are an indication of your confusion and need to understand. Death is incomprehensible. It doesn't make sense, perhaps because, deep down, there is an innate knowledge that death is an enemy. It was never meant to be. Whatever the cause, then, you must acknowledge your anger, accept it as a normal human emotion, and find some constructive outlet. And don't be afraid to share your feelings with a sympathetic friend, as well as with God. Talking about anger, rather than letting it build up inside, is an essential step towards dealing with it, and using it for good.

Guilt

Another common feeling associated with grief is guilt. This tends to be false guilt, which means that it has no legitimate cause: you have done nothing wrong. But it can feel very real and lead to self-condemnatory thoughts that go round and round in your head, leading nowhere. You may, for instance, feel guilty because you didn't urge your loved one to seek medical help sooner, for failing to be there at the moment of death, or because you were never able to express loving thoughts and feelings. Conversely, you might feel guilty because of things you did say in moments of stress, giving them a significance they don't actually warrant. You might even go so far as to think that your words or actions brought about the death. This is especially likely if you have suffered a miscarriage or stillbirth, or lost someone through suicide.

If the deceased suffered a lot of pain, or caused you a lot of pain, you are likely to feel guilty for being relieved when death finally occurred. And if your beloved died as a result of an accident or disaster in which you also were involved, you will probably feel guilty for having survived. But even with the closest of relationships and the most peaceful of endings, you might feel guilty for being able to smile and laugh again, or for enjoying again the beauty of the world around. However, like the surges of hurt and anger, these feelings also are a normal part of grieving, and not at all unusual. Knowing this will enable you to talk back to yourself, reminding yourself that your guilt is unwarranted, and that it will pass.

If you know that you actually did fail the deceased in some way, then you must forgive yourself. We all do things we regret, but we can learn from our mistakes and so become better people:

humbler, wiser and far more loving and gentle. This would surely be the best way to make amends, far more constructive than tormenting yourself with futile recriminations. It might help to talk to your pastor or priest about your guilt feelings, and the reasons for them; and, of course, to confess any shortcomings to God. He, above all else, understands and is ready to forgive, so that he can come alongside, to comfort you in your loneliness and fear.

Loneliness and Fear

When you have lost someone, especially a partner with whom you shared a loving relationship, you are bound to feel sad and lonely. And it often comes as a shock every time the realisation hits that there is no one there to talk to any more with such openness and trust. But the loneliness of grief comes also from feeling that a part of you is missing, or even that you have been disconnected, shut up in a glass cage where no one can reach you. However supportive your family and friends are, that sense of being incomplete or cut off can make you wonder at times if you will ever again feel like a normal functioning member of the human race. And this exacerbates the very common but odd sensation that you are standing still, while the rest of the world moves on.

Following a bereavement, it is not unusual to look at the world around and wonder why it doesn't stop. You might, for instance, look at a tree laden with spring blossom or bright with the colours of autumn and be amazed that it can be so beautiful when, for you, life has ended. Or you might look up into a sunny blue sky and think it all wrong that it isn't black and heavy with rain. You could find yourself watching people shopping in the High Street, or children playing, and feel that there is something unnatural about their carrying on as usual. And your bewilderment will make you feel more than ever that you have been left stranded, an alien in a strange new world.

These distorted perceptions can be very frightening, and they add to all the other fears that surface when you have been left alone in the world. Some will be old fears, perhaps in a different guise; others will be untypical, making you wonder what on earth is happening to you. You might, for instance, be suddenly afraid of being in the house alone, of driving to work, or handling the finances. You might become overly anxious about your own health or the health of your children, and even become obsessed with frightening thoughts of your own demise, especially if your children are young and still dependent on you. And naturally, you will be afraid of facing a future without your loved one. But, when the time is right, you will once again feel that you are not alone, that you are reconnected with the rest of the human race, and that you are moving on to better and happier times.

COPING WITH GRIEF

Come Aside

The feeling of being marooned on a desert island or banished into the wilderness, far from being an aberration, is essential in the early stages of grieving. You need this time apart, cocooned in your own little world, in order to readjust. But this doesn't mean that you physically shut yourself away from everyone; rather, it means that you allow yourself a transitional period in which you can say goodbye. This is not the time to make major decisions about moving or changing jobs, or to start planning new ventures. This is a time to mourn. If you are one of those people who just get on with things no matter what life throws at you, or feel that you have to be the strong one in the family and look after everyone else, then you will have to work harder at giving yourself permission to grieve. You are human too, and must attend to your own needs so that you can let go of the past. Only then can you truly begin to reach out for the new and interesting things that life still has to offer.

The funeral normally marks the beginning of this letting go. But sometimes, even long afterwards, there can be a disturbing feeling of something having been left unfinished. You might, for instance, feel that you need to go back and spend more time with the deceased, speaking your thoughts or holding the body, even though this is now impossible. This often happens following a neonatal death, partly because of not having been

14

able to get to know the baby in the first place. And if you rushed away because you experienced the very common fear that the baby might disintegrate in your arms, your longing will be exacerbated by a tendency to self-condemnation. It is important, therefore, that you find some way of mentally putting things right, perhaps by arranging a special farewell visit to the grave or crematorium, having a commemorative service, or by getting out

photographs or belongings you have pushed away out of sight and spending time alone with your memories. Above all, do talk to someone about the way you are feelings, and give voice to your questions and doubts. Don't keep them bottled up inside.

Following a death questions usually arise, perhaps for the first time, about God and the meaning of existence. This mental probing is important. But, as with everything else, you must not rush into anything while your mind is disturbed and you are desperate for answers. Instead, give yourself time and space to search, reflect and make sense of what is happening to you. If you are a committed Christian, this period could be one in which you experience a new closeness with God. On the other hand, you might find that your faith has been badly shaken. This is more likely if, in the past, you accepted everything without question. But you needn't be alarmed. True faith can stand up to being tested and, in time, you will discover that, although your beliefs might not be as black-and-white as formerly, your faith will have grown deeper, richer and far more meaningful.

Keep Going

While you are allowing yourself the calm and stillness necessary to come to terms with your loss, you must also keep going. After the initial phase of numbness and disbelief there is often a period of hyperactivity, caused by the surge of adrenalin that is activated by stress. But then, as the stress level subsides, you will find that you can hardly summon up enough energy to just keep things ticking over. If you have young children to look after, this period is likely to be very draining, so you will need to pace yourself and concentrate on essentials. And this includes taking care of your own needs.

Hopefully your friends will have remained in contact, so do accept their invitations for coffee or offers of practical help. And, without overdoing it, ensure that you have plenty of fresh air and exercise. In the early days, when your energy level is at its lowest, you might find that all you can manage is an occasional short walk round the block. So start with this, and gradually push yourself further until you are able to take on more vigorous activities, like dancing, aerobics, or some kind of sport. Any kind of exercise will give your spirits a temporary boost, and help get you through the day, because it releases endorphins – natural painkillers – in the brain. Later on, if you don't already have some employment, paid or otherwise, perhaps you could get involved in voluntary work, join a church or club, take up a hobby or attend an evening class. Meanwhile, do ensure that you eat healthily and continue to take an interest in your appearance. And, while looking after your material needs, don't forget your soul – the thinking/feeling part of the self that is concerned with life and creativity.

The soul needs space in which to develop and grow, and it thrives on beauty, as well as goodness and truth. Therefore, in order to speed your recovery from the feeling of depression that follows bereavement, you must feed your soul on the things it craves. Take time, then, to look around you at the beauty of creation, however strange and out of keeping it might seem with your general mood. Take yourself into the country and experience the soothing loveliness of rivers and meadows, the fresh wildness of moorland or the primeval peace of the forests. If you live near the sea, walking along the beach can be very uplifting. Or perhaps you would prefer the ordered tranquillity of formal gardens, or the reassuring sense of history that is felt in old churches, stately homes and among the ruins of ancient castles. These activities will not only meet your aesthetic needs, but also help you attain a sense of the greatness and wonder of creation, so enabling you to put your loss in perspective and make it more manageable.

Reach Out

Following a bereavement, you will want to spend a lot of time alone. And, as has been said, it is important that you have this time for yourself, communing with your own soul as well as with God. But you also need to reach out to other people. Although grief is very private, no two people experiencing it the same, it is universal. And there will be friends who will understand the pain of grief and respond appropriately, with care and sensitivity. So don't be afraid to talk about the one you have lost or to verbalise your thoughts and feelings, no matter how disturbing or irrational they might seem. If the deceased was someone who persistently hurt you, this also needs to come out in the open, so that you can become free of painful or shameful memories. Similarly, if you have been badly traumatised by your loved one's death, talk about it. And keep on talking until you are no longer tormented by recurring mental images of violence and destruction.

When there is a need to talk about the same thing over and over, friends can become overburdened. And although they may be able to provide support and a listening ear, they will probably not be able to help you work through the pain of abuse, or the experience of losing someone through suicide or any other act of violence, which includes traffic accidents, homicide, terrorist attack or environmental disaster. In these cases it is advisable to seek help from a counsellor or psychotherapist who will be able to give you the skilled assistance required. There may be a counsellor at your GP practice. Otherwise, you can find details in Yellow Pages, or through contacting a professional organisation, such as ACC (Association of Christian Counsellors) or BACP (British Association for Counselling and Psychotherapy). You might also find it beneficial to join a group that specialises in helping the bereaved, such as Cruse, the National Association of Bereavement Services, or the Stillbirth and Neonatal Death Society.

Whether or not you avail yourself of professional assistance or join a support group, it is essential that you remain in contact with your friends, and that you keep them informed of your needs. Many people really want to help, but they don't know how. And usually they are grateful for any guidance you can give them. But perhaps you also have only a confused sense of what your needs are, or have difficulty articulating them. In this case, you will find the next section particularly helpful. You might want to share it with interested friends, to enable them to provide the best possible support as they accompany you on your journey to recovery.

HOW FRIENDS CAN HELP

Being There

You may have discovered, on losing your loved one, that the friends you expected to be supportive started avoiding you. This, unfortunately, happens very frequently, not because they don't care, but because they don't know what to say. It is also common for mothers of young children to stop inviting a newly bereaved friend to their home because they are afraid of their children mentioning the deceased or asking awkward questions. But their actions are misguided. You need to be around people. And they don't actually need to say anything. What really matters is their concern. A look of sympathy, eyes that well with shared tears, a hug and, above all, the ability to listen, all give the clear and comforting message, "You are not alone in this. I am here."

The tendency of friends to avoid comes in part from today's attitude to death. It has almost become a taboo subject. It isn't talked about. The rituals that enabled people to cope with death have largely been abandoned. And, unlike those of earlier generations, few today have experienced a death first hand. The terminally ill tend to die in hospital, rather than at home, cared for by trained professionals — which does, of course, have its advantages. But when you have been bereaved, you need to talk, not only about the one you have lost, but about death itself: the last hours, your feelings about being in the presence of death, questions about death.... And you need to cry. It is more hurtful to have friends studiously avoiding mentioning the deceased than it is to have them, or their children, asking questions or making comments that cause you to dissolve into tears.

When family and friends are able to be there, it is usually in the first few weeks following a death. But, as has been noted, it is after this period, when the shock and numbness have worn off, that you need them most. And if you have lost a spouse or partner, or someone else close to you, you will continue to need their support years later. You might only require the comfort of knowing there is someone you can turn to on the bad days, when

you are missing your beloved more than usual, or when painful memories have been triggered by an anniversary or some other recollection of the deceased. It is reassuring, therefore, if your friends periodically remind you, through phone calls, cards or letters, that they are still thinking about you.

Providing Assistance

In the early days especially, you will also need your friends to help out practically. If you are the kind of person who is always running around looking after everyone else, you might find it difficult to be on the receiving end for a change. But this is not a sign of weakness or inadequacy. On the contrary! The ability to humbly and gratefully accept aid from others, as well as giving it, is an indication of a healthy self-esteem. But also bear in mind that, following a death, your sense of self will be somewhat shaky, and you might want to protect yourself from feeling too dependent. Nevertheless, as well as requiring assistance with the funeral arrangements, you will at first also need help with the general running of the household. Your friends could perhaps take over some of the routine chores, provide meals, babysit, or ferry your children to and from school. You might also need support and advice as you sort out the finances or go through your loved one's possessions, deciding what to keep and what to pass on.

If you have young children who have lost a parent or sibling, friends can assist you in answering their many questions about death and dying, and provide support as you help your little ones to say goodbye. If children want to attend the funeral, they should not be excluded, and right there your friends can make it easier for you by keeping an eye on them, distracting them if necessary, and generally keeping them occupied. Later on, your friends can help by taking your children to the cemetery or crematorium on those days when you really cannot cope with explaining, yet again, why the deceased has gone to live with Jesus, why the body was buried or the ashes scattered, what the nice new body is like.... It will also take some of the pressure off you if friends spend time with your children, doing the kind of fun things that you will not at first be able to face.

As time passes, you will be increasingly able to cope on your own, especially if your friends have gently encouraged you to be independent. But long after the death there might be things that you cannot manage entirely alone, such as gardening, moving furniture, or carrying out household repairs. If you are elderly or disabled you might need help with transport or shopping, claiming benefits or obtaining assistance from social services. But whatever your age, and however well you are coping, it is always comforting to receive some practical recognition of your ongoing struggles, such as a home-made cake or a gift of fruit or flowers, especially if they are given with sensitivity and tact.

Being Sensitive

Although it is not essential for friends to come up with exactly the right words in their attempts to comfort you, it is important that they have some understanding of the devastating effect of losing someone close to you, and that they are sensitive to your changing emotions. Well-meaning people have been known to say the most hurtful things following a bereavement, such as, "You're doing so well", "It's probably for the best", or most commonly, "I know just how you feel". These, rather than helping, make the bereaved feel alienated because of the very obvious lack of empathy. What you really need are friends who can tune into *your* feelings and sense what the loss means to *you*. And this includes recognising, and in some way acknowledging, that no one can replace or compensate for the one you have lost.

The Bible tells us that, "A word aptly spoken is like apples of gold in settings of silver". [1] It is a comfort indeed if you have friends who think carefully about their words and how they might affect you, fitting them to the occasion. And the very fact that they have struggled to get it right, even if they didn't quite succeed, is an indication of their love and concern. Friends like these will also know how to be there without being intrusive or making you feel that you are a burden. And they will be aware of their own limitations and be able to set boundaries. It is important for you — and for them — to have these boundaries, in order to feel safe. You must be told if your needs are excessive or require more specialised help and, when appropriate, be directed towards those who can provide it. This will prevent a lot of unnecessary suffering. And, through their timely interventions, you will experience more fully the healing that comes from being truly loved and cared for.

HEALING AND HOPE

Hope Springs Eternal

Just as the body can heal itself, so can the soul. And with the right kind of care, the natural healing of this life-giving, creative part of the self is enhanced, and hope revives. It seems that, deep within us, we have an innate ability to believe that there are better times ahead, both in this life and in the world to come. However, if there has been severe trauma in the early years and the wounds go deep, this natural resilience is impaired, making recovery from any subsequent loss slower and more difficult. This is why, if you are stuck in the depressed stage of grief and continue to feel that there is no hope for the future, you ideally need professional help, not only to cope with your recent bereavement, but to also receive treatment for neglected injuries from the past.

As the wounds, past and present, begin to heal, you will again start to take an interest in the world around you and want to venture out: to meet new people, learn new skills. You may even find yourself wanting to do things you have often contemplated but never had the freedom, money or courage to try, and this is a good time to seize the opportunity. You could, for example, start a long-dreamed-of university course, find a more interesting job with better prospects, or begin a new business venture. You might want to move house, travel, learn a new language.... The possibilities are endless. In the early stages of grief you could only live from one day to the next. But now it is important that you have long-term, as well as short-term, goals, and that you start reaching towards them, believing that one day you will realise your dreams.

In addition to the hope deep within us that life will always

have something to offer, we also have an innate knowledge that death is not the end. This is not surprising because we have evidence of this everywhere we look. Year after year, after the deadness of winter when it seemed that nothing would ever grow and blossom again, spring returns. Then, once again, fresh grass springs up in the meadows, primroses cover the banks, celandine lines the footpaths, and the green woods thrill with the fragrant promise of unending vistas of bluebells. This miracle of new life in nature points us to Christ, the Son of God, who died at Easter – the time of the Spring Equinox – and rose again, that we might have eternal life.

This hope of eternal life means that we can also hope to see our loved ones again. If the one you have lost was a known believer in Christ's resurrection power, then you have something very solid and comforting to hold onto – although this does not mean that you will bypass the normal grieving process. Christians grieve too, but not as those who have no hope. [2] If you are not certain of the deceased's standing in God, this will naturally add to your grief. And yet, you can comfort yourself with the thought that, to some degree, we all have an innate sense of the divine. [3] And sometimes those who have made no profession of faith have a deep perception of the spiritual. The dying process itself enhances this awareness, and even in unconsciousness there are stirrings of the soul that are not always evident to outside observers. The thief dying on the cross beside Christ, recognising him as the Son of God, asked in his final hours to be remembered. And Jesus assured him that, before the day was out, they would meet in paradise. [4]

Love Never Dies

Hope and faith never die, and neither does love, which is the greatest of the three. [5] Your loved one may have passed on, but the love remains, not only in your thoughts and memories, but also in your very soul. Throughout life we are constantly internalising – taking in – our experience of other people and, consciously or otherwise, integrating their thoughts, feelings and attributes with our own. The closer we are to someone, the more they become part of us, as we become part of them. So, if you had a positive experience of the deceased, at some point in the grieving process you will have a sudden comforting awareness

that he or she is somehow there, inside you, loving and cherishing you, in death as in life.

If, on the other hand, your memories of the deceased are painful ones, you should not try to blot them out, but rather work through them. This means facing up to them, allowing the feelings to surface and finding some constructive outlet for them; then, through an act of forgiveness, letting them go. This does not mean accepting or excusing any mistreatment, but giving up the futile desire for revenge or restitution. This will also enable you to get rid of any negative aspects of the other that you have incorporated into your own psyche and that are holding you back. Forgiveness is an act of love, and it is so much easier when you are able to open yourself up to love, from other people as well as from God.

Love is very powerful, and the more you experience it, the more you will be able to give. And the more you can give, the greater will be your hope for the future. Grief can seem as if it will go on forever. But you *will* live through it. Then, as life becomes rich and fulfilling again, with a new meaning and purpose, you will know assuredly that nothing can destroy love — not even death.

Scripture References

1   Proverbs 25: 11
2   1 Thessalonians 4: 13
3   Ecclesiastes 3: 11
4   Luke 23: 42-43
5   1 Corinthians 13: 13

WORDS OF COMFORT

A time to mourn

There is a time for everything, and a season for every activity under heaven: a time to be born and a time to die...a time to weep and a time to laugh, a time to mourn and a time to dance ....

(Ecclesiastes 3:1-4)

Blessed are those who mourn, for they will be comforted.

(Matthew 5:4)

Blessed are you who weep now, for you will laugh.   *(Luke 6:21)*

God our comfort

He heals the broken-hearted and binds up their wounds.

(Psalm 147:3)

I, even I, am he who comforts you.   *(Isaiah 51:12)*

As a mother comforts her child, so will I comfort you....

(Isaiah 66:13)

Praise be to the God and Father of our Lord Jesus Christ, the Father of compassion and the God of all comfort, who comforts us in all our troubles, so that we can comfort those in any trouble with the comfort we ourselves have received from God.

(2 Corinthians 1:3-4)

Resurrection hope

For God so loved the world that he gave his one and only Son, that whoever believes in him shall not perish but have eternal life.

(John 3:16)

Jesus said to her [Martha], "I am the resurrection and the life. He who believes in me will live, even though he dies...."

(John 11:25)

Death destroyed

He will swallow up death for ever. The Sovereign Lord will wipe away the tears from all faces.... *(Isaiah 25:8)*

The last enemy to be destroyed is death. *(1 Corinthians 15:26)*

When the perishable has been clothed with the imperishable, and the mortal with immortality, then the saying that is written will come true: "Death has been swallowed up in victory."
> "Where, O death, is your victory?
> Where, O death, is your sting?"

(1 Corinthians 15:54-55)

This grace was given us in Christ Jesus before the beginning of time, but it has now been revealed through the appearing of our Saviour, Christ Jesus, who has destroyed death and has brought life and immortality to light through the gospel. *(2 Timothy 1:10)*

He will wipe every tear from their eyes. There will be no more death or mourning or crying or pain, for the old order of things has passed away. *(Revelation 21:4)*

Love never fails

For the Lord is good and his love endures for ever; his faithfulness continues through all generations. *(Psalm 100: 5)*

For I am convinced that neither death nor life, neither angels nor demons, neither the present nor the future, nor any powers, neither height nor depth, nor anything else in all creation, will be able to separate us from the love of God that is in Christ Jesus our Lord. *(Romans 8:38-39)*

It [love] always protects, always trusts, always hopes, always perseveres. Love never fails. *(1 Corinthians 13:7-8)*

Also by Jennifer Minney

Self-esteem: The way of humility

This thoughtful book promotes the development of self-esteem on the basis of one's identity in God, through creation and redemption. This foundation, it explains, is essential for creating a respect for self that is humble and grateful, and that leads to a more responsible and effective stewardship of one's gifts and abilities.

The author, a counsellor with a BA (Hons) in Psychology, and more than twenty years experience of helping people with low self-esteem, draws also on her Bible college, nursing and midwifery training to explore and discuss five aspects of the self: body, soul, spirit, heart and mind. With each, there is a survey of common misconceptions and problems, with guidelines for overcoming them.

£5.95   **ISBN: 0-9538446-2-5**

Will Jesus kick my ball back?

The amazing story of an adoption that should have been impossible, of cerebral palsy, and a child whose avid curiosity and irrepressible giggles have made him a joy to many.

It is also the story of the author's spiritual and psychological journey, from a background of abuse and rejection, through years of infertility, to a place of trust in God's goodness, even when his long-promised child turns out to be severely brain-damaged.

The two stories blend as mother and child grow together, developing their full potential as she learns to love herself and a child whom a neurologist had written off.

This book has had a profound impact on those who have read it, provoking laughter, producing tears, challenging and uplifting. It is a book that is hard to put down.

£6.95   **ISBN: 0-9538446-0-9**

Beyond depression: Growing into light
ISBN: 0-9538446-3-3

Beyond fear: Growing into faith
ISBN: 0-9538446-5-X

Beyond stress: Growing into serenity
ISBN: 0-9538446-4-1

Each of the above titles in the *Grobook* series discusses the signs and symptoms of common emotional problems, the current triggers and deep-rooted causes, and provides guidelines for overcoming the immediate effects. Using Bible characters as case studies, the difficulties are also viewed in the context of the entire person, and the reader is helped to find healing from past traumas and begin changing destructive patterns of thinking and behaviour; to move beyond the problem towards spiritual and psychological wholeness.
All titles £3.50

Song of Creation
An illustrated collection of poems, grouped according to the seven days of creation, and celebrating life in all its varied forms. Many of the poems have a Celtic flavour, and they range from the light-hearted to the deeply spiritual.

There are poems for every mood and need. For example, there is the reassuring "Dark Night of the Soul", the bracing "Sea Longing", the mystical "Forest Whispers", the exuberant "Fun Fishes" and the restful "By Quiet Waters". Each day of creation is introduced with the relevant quotation from Genesis, and there is a thought-provoking section on current environmental issues — creation in danger. This is an anthology you will want to read again and again. Suitable also for use in church services, youth groups, women's meetings, etc.
Price to be announced   **ISBN: 0-9538446-1-7**

All Silvertree titles are available from bookshops or can be purchased (postage free in UK) direct from:

Silvertree Publishing
PO Box 2768
Yeovil
Somerset BA22 8XZ

Become a Silvertree Book Agent

If you found this book helpful, why not become a Silvertree Book Agent, and so benefit others whilst also earning money for yourself, your church, or your favourite charity?

For full details, send an s.a.e. to the above address.